A Note to Parents and Teachers

DK READERS is a compelling program for beginning readers, designed in conjunction with leading literacy experts, including Dr. Linda Gambrell, director of the Eugene T. Moore School of Education at Clemson University. Dr. Gambrell has served on the Board of Directors of the International Reading Association and as president of the National Reading Conference.

Beautiful illustrations and superb full-color photographs combine with engaging, easy-to-read stories to offer a fresh approach to each subject in the series. Each DK READER is guaranteed to capture a child's interest while developing his or her reading skills, general knowledge, and love of reading.

The five levels of DK READERS are aimed at different reading abilities, enabling you to choose the books that are exactly right for your children:

Pre-Level 1 – Learning to read
Level 1 – Beginning to read
Level 2 – Beginning to read alone
Level 3 – Reading alone
Level 4 – Proficient readers

The "normal" age at which a child begins to read can be anywhere from three to eight years old, so these levels are only a general guideline.

No matter which level you select, you can be sure that you are helping your child learn to read, then read to learn!

LONDON, NEW YORK, MELBOURNE,
MUNICH, AND DELHI

Senior Editor Beth Sutinis
Editor Elizabeth Hester
Designer Tai Blanche
Assistant Managing Art Editor Michelle Baxter
Jacket Art Director Dirk Kaufman
DTP Designer Milos Orlovic
Production Chris Avgherinos

Reading Consultant
Linda Gambrell, Ph.D.

Produced by
Shoreline Publishing Group
Editorial Director James Buckley, Jr.
Art Director Tom Carling
Carling Design, Inc.

Produced in partnership and licensed by
Major League Baseball Properties, Inc.
**Vice President of Publishing
and MLB Photos** Don Hintze

First American Edition, 2004
04 05 06 07 08 09 10 9 8 7 6 5 4 3 2 1
Published in the United States by DK Publishing, Inc.
375 Hudson St., New York, NY 10014

Published in Great Britain by Dorling Kindersley Limited.

A catalog record for this book is available from the Library of Congress.
ISBN: 0-7566-0839-2 (PB)
0-7566-0836-8 (HC)

Color reproduction by Colourscan, Singapore
Printed and bound in China by L Rex Printing Co., Ltd.

Photography credits:
(t: top; b: bottom; l: left; r: right)
AP/Wide World: 10b, 14b, 15tb, 17b, 23b, 28tb, 30tb, 37tb, 42l; Corbis: 5r, 7b, 11b,
12b, 16tb, 23r, 24b, 27, 29, 31, 36tl, 38tb, 46b; DK Library/Shoreline Publishing Group:
25tr, 35tr, 36bl; Courtesy Mastronet (www.mastronet.com): 14t, 41br; National
Baseball Hall of Fame and Library: 6b, 7b, 9r, 11br, 18t, 24b, 26b, 41t, 46tl;
Northeastern University World Series Museum: 44b; Transcendental Graphics: 6t, 22tl.

Discover more at
www.dk.com

Contents

Birth of the Series   4

1912: Early classic   6

1960: Imagine that   10

1975: Picture this   16

1986: Curses!   24

1991: Cinderella story   32

2001: Goliath falls   40

Glossary   48

OCTOBER MAGIC

Written by Jim Gigliotti

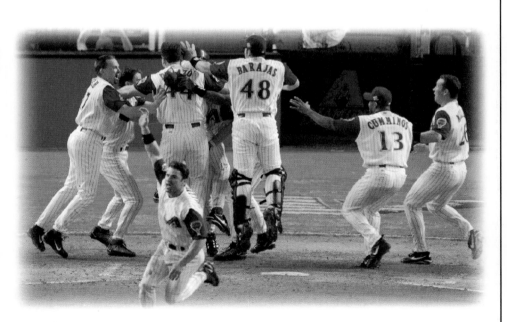

DK Publishing, Inc.

Antique ball
This baseball was used in the first World Series, which was played in 1903 between Pittsburg and Boston.

The prize
The World Series Trophy is presented to the best team in baseball each October.

Birth of the Series

In 1903, the Pittsburg Pirates (they didn't use the "h" then) of the National League (N.L.) challenged the Boston Americans of the American League (A.L.) to a series to determine baseball's best team. The World Series was born.

The Americans, representing a league that had begun only two years earlier, surprised most baseball observers by taking that first Series from their more seasoned opponents. They won five games to three (the best-of-nine series was later changed to the current best-of-seven).

Ever since that surprise beginning, the World Series has continued to provide fans with unexpected, even amazing, thrills. What follows in this book are a few of those magical stories.

There's the kind of magic where a Red Sox player waves his arms to

encourage a home run ball to stay fair . . . where a Mets' team one strike away from losing comes back for an extraordinary victory . . . where two last-place teams from the season before play one of the most exciting World Series in history. And where an expansion team comes out of nowhere to beat the most storied team in all of sports.

It's the kind of magic that is October Magic.

Magical moment
The young Florida Marlins made the 2003 playoffs as a wild-card team, then upset the favored New York Yankees in the World Series, winning four games to two.

1912: Early classic

The World Series was still in its formative years in 1912.

The competition had begun only nine years earlier, in 1903.

Already, though, the World Series had produced its share of memorable moments. Some had come on the mound, like when Christy Mathewson pitched three shutouts for the N.L.'s New York Giants in 1905. Some were at the plate: Frank Baker cemented his reputation as "Home Run Baker" for the A.L.'s Philadelphia Athletics in 1911. One came off the field: In 1904, Giants manager John McGraw refused to play the A.L.'s Boston Americans!

But to really capture America's attention, the World Series needed a great series of games. In 1912, the World Series finally had it all.

Get your program!
This souvenir from the 1912 World Series cost only 10 cents.

Series star
Giants ace Christy Mathewson was one of the earliest Series stars. He tossed three shutouts against the Athletics in 1905.

There were heroes and goats, timely pitching and clutch hitting, and several tight games that ended with a thrilling finale. To this day, the Boston Red Sox' four-games-to-three triumph over the Giants remains one of the most exciting Series in history.

Smokey Joe "There's no man alive who can throw the ball harder than Smokey Joe Wood," legendary pitcher Walter Johnson said.

Righthander-in-Chief President William Howard Taft threw out the ceremonial first pitch on Opening Day of 1912.

Blame game
Outfielder Fred Snodgrass (below) is often cited as the scapegoat in the Giants' Game-Eight loss for his famous muff in the 10th inning, but a misplayed foul pop was just as damaging.

The 1912 Series actually lasted eight games instead of seven. Game Two was called a 6–6 tie after 11 innings because of darkness.

Ace starter Smokey Joe Wood, who had won 34 games and lost only five during the regular season, won two more games as the Red Sox built a three-games-to-one lead.

But the Giants stayed alive by winning two, even knocking Wood out early in an 11–4 rout in the seventh game. That win set up a Game-Eight finale in Boston. The Giants' Mathewson and the Red Sox' Hugh Bedient battled through seven innings with the score tied at 1–1. Wood came on in the eighth inning,

GIANTS

NY

Fred Snodgrass

OF THE
NEW YORK NATIONALS

but neither team scored until New York pushed across a run in the top of the 10th.

In the bottom of the 10th, Giants center fielder Fred Snodgrass dropped a routine fly ball to open the inning. Though Snodgrass made a fantastic catch on the next play, the tying run moved to third base with one out. After a walk, Boston outfielder Tris Speaker lofted a lazy foul ball that Mathewson, first baseman Fred Merkle, and catcher Chief Meyers let drop between them. The two misplays were too much. Given a reprieve, Speaker lined a tying single. Soon after, Larry Gardner's sacrifice fly won it, 4–3. The Red Sox were World Series champions!

Big stick
Red Sox outfielder Tris Speaker batted .383 in 1912 and had the key hit in the 10th inning of the final game of the World Series.

"Big Train"
Another great World Series in the early days came in 1924, when pitcher Walter Johnson (left) carried the Washington Senators past the Giants in seven games.

9

Bronx Bomber
Mickey Mantle hit three home runs in the Series for the Yankees, but it wasn't enough for his team to overcome the Pirates.

Star on the rise
Young Pirates oufielder Roberto Clemente (right) hit .310 in his first World Series.

1960: Imagine that

If you ever picked up a ball and a glove, and especially if you've ever held a bat in your hands, you've almost certainly dreamed of hitting the home run that wins the World Series.

Maybe your dream was in the park, or the schoolyard, or your very own backyard, but it's sounded the same: "Game Seven of the World Series. Bottom of the ninth inning, potential winning run at the plate. Here's the pitch. There's a long drive. It could be…It is! Home run! And the crowd goes wild!" You circle the bases as fans pour out of the stands. At home plate, you are mobbed by your teammates. It would be a dream come true.

It was just such a scenario that ended the 1960 World Series in a dramatic way. Pittsburgh second baseman Bill Mazeroski launched a solo home run leading off the bottom of the ninth inning of the final game of the Series. Mazeroski's blast gave the Pirates a 10–9 victory over the New York Yankees in that memorable Game Seven, and it gave Pittsburgh a four-games-to-three triumph in the Series.

Tools of the trade
At the Baseball Hall of Fame, you can see the helmet, bat, and glove Mazeroski used in the 1960 World Series.

Hero in Hall
Thanks to a great career beyond this one magical game, Bill Mazeroski was elected to the Hall of Fame as a player in 2001.

Decisive blast
Toronto's Joe Carter ended the 1993 Series against Philadelphia with a three-run home run in the ninth inning of Game Six.

Remember, the Series had begun way back in 1903. Believe it or not, it was the first time that a walk-off home run ended the World Series. It is still the only time that a home run has ended Game Seven.

Even before Mazeroski's home run, the 1960 World Series was one to remember. It offered a remarkable contrast between the heavy-hitting Yankees, who romped to victory in each of their three wins, and the scrappy Pirates, who eked out their four victories by a combined total of seven runs.

As a team, the Yankees batted .338 in the Series. They had 27 extra-base hits, including 10 home runs. They won Game Two in a 16–3 rout, Game Three by a 10–0 score, and Game Six by 12–0. Whitey Ford pitched both of the shutouts, but the real story was New York's hitters. Outfielder Mickey

Mantle slugged two home runs in the second game, and second baseman Bobby Richardson hit a grand slam and drove in a record six runs in the third game. For the Series, catcher Elston Howard hit .462, while Mantle batted .400. Richardson hit .367 and set another Series record with 12 runs batted in.

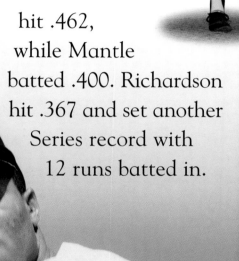

Ace starter
Whitey Ford got plenty of run support, though he didn't need it while pitching two shutouts.

Heavy hitter
Catcher Elston Howard (left) and his teammates feasted on the Pirates' pitching, but it wasn't enough for the Yankees to win the Series.

13

Almost home
Pirates second baseman Bill Mazeroski (right) is about to touch the plate with the winning run in the 1960 Series.

Autographed ball
Hall of Famers Yogi Berra and Mickey Mantle are among the Yankees whose signatures are on this baseball.

The Pirates, meanwhile, batted just .256 in the Series. They hit only four home runs, and they had to claw their way to victories of 6–4 in Game One, 3–2 in Game Four, and 5–2 in Game Five. Game Seven was at Pittsburgh's Forbes Field.

It was a see-saw affair which began with the hometown Pirates jumping to a 4–0 lead after two innings. The Yankees battled back, though, and took a seemingly safe 7–4 advantage in the eighth inning. But the Pirates produced a five-run uprising by Pittsburgh that was capped by catcher Hal Smith's three-run home run for a 9–7 lead. Still, the Yankees weren't done yet. They rallied again with two runs in the top of the ninth inning to tie the game at 9–9.

Mazeroski led off the Pirates' half of the ninth and took the first pitch from New York's Ralph Terry for a ball. Then Mazeroski deposited the second pitch over the wall in left field. He gleefully skipped around the bases. Fans poured out of the stands. At home plate, "Maz" was mobbed by his teammates. It was a dream come true.

Winning pitcher
Harvey Haddix won 1960's famous Game Seven for the Pirates.

Mr. October
The Yankees' Reggie Jackson hit three home runs on three successive swings in New York's Series clincher against the Dodgers in 1977.

1975: Picture this

Sports has a way of engraving lasting images in our memories. Maybe you are old enough to remember Michael Jordan sinking a game-winning jumper for the Chicago Bulls. Or maybe your snapshots include Brett Favre throwing a winning touchdown pass for the Green Bay Packers. Or Jeff Gordon winning a big stock-car race. Every sports fan has a personal scrapbook of memories in the mind.

For baseball fans, one of the most famous images is that of catcher Carlton Fisk hitting a game-winning home run for the A.L.'s Boston Red Sox against the N.L.'s Cincinnati Reds in Game Six of the 1975 World Series.

Winning images
We all remember our favorite sports moments, like a game-winning jumper from the Chicago Bulls' Michael Jordan (above) or a touchdown pass from the Green Bay Packers' Brett Favre (below).

The Reds and Red Sox gave baseball fans nearly nonstop excitement that year. Game Six was one of the greatest single games ever. The Red Sox won that battle. But the Reds won the war, taking the Series in seven games.

Little Joe
Gritty second baseman Joe Morgan (above, center) won two games in the Series, including the finale, with hits in the Reds' last at-bat.

Hero's welcome Catcher Carlton Fisk (27, left) is greeted at home plate by his Red Sox teammates after hitting the winning home run in the 12th inning of Game Six.

Bench-marks
Cincinnati's Johnny Bench set the hitting standard for all big-league catchers.

Winning run
The Reds' Dave Concepcion scores a run in the last inning of Game Two.

Cincinnati's "Big Red Machine" was favored to win the 1975 Series. Manager Sparky Anderson's powerful lineup included Johnny Bench (who was perhaps the greatest hitting catcher of all time), outfielder George Foster, first baseman Tony Perez, and second baseman Joe Morgan.

Boston was led by rookie outfielder Fred Lynn, who batted .331, and pitcher Luis Tiant, who had won 18 games in the regular season.

Tiant, a Cuban-born right hander nicknamed "El Tiante," had a unique pitching delivery. To begin each wind-up, he turned his body as if looking at something in center field, aiming his back to the plate, before twisting all the way around to throw toward home. Using this unique motion, he baffled many hitters.

Reds' uprising
The only relatively easy victory for the Reds came in Game Five, when Tony Perez (left) homered twice to spark Cincinnati's 6–2 win.

El Tiante
Right hander Luis Tiant won 20 or more games three times for the Red Sox in the 1970s.

The Reds' hitters never could adjust to Tiant in Game One and lost 6–0. In Game Two, Reds' Dave Concepcion and Ken Griffey drove in the tying and winning runs with two-out hits in the ninth inning. Five of the last six games would be decided by one run.

Grand theft Boston's Dwight Evans was out at home plate in Game One (right). In Game Six, he reached into stands to take away a home run and keep the Red Sox' hopes alive.

Sparky's men Manager George "Sparky" Anderson led the Big Red Machine to back-to-back World Series wins in 1975 and 1976.

Tiant won Game Four with a complete game, but the Reds took a three-games-to-two lead with a 6–2 win in Game Five. Game Six at Fenway Park was unforgettable. Because rain delayed the game for three days, Tiant took the mound for Boston again. Lynn staked him to a lead by hitting a three-run home run in the first. But this time, the Red Sox' ace couldn't hold the advantage. Cincinnati finally knocked Tiant out of the game after taking a 6–3 lead in the top of the eighth inning.

However, with two outs in the bottom of the eighth inning, Boston's Bernie Carbo hit a dramatic, three-run, pinch-hit home run to tie the game. The fans in Fenway Park went crazy! Three innings later, they were on their feet again when right fielder Dwight Evans reached into the stands to rob Morgan of a home run.

Instant impact
In 1975, Red Sox outfielder Fred Lynn (19) became the first player to win rookie of the year and most valuable player honors in the same season. He batted .331 that year and drove in 105 runs.

Then in the bottom of the 12th, with the game still tied 6–6, Fisk led off for the Red Sox. The first pitch was a ball. Fisk lofted the second one high and deep to left. It was long enough—there was no doubt about that. But was it fair or foul? "Stay fair! Stay fair!" Fisk screamed.

The ball banged off the screen of the foul pole. Home run! Boston won, 7–6, and evened the Series.

It was past midnight the morning of October 22 when

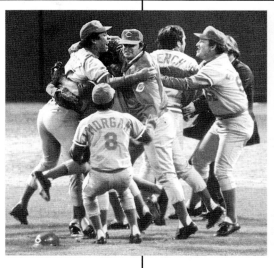

the emotional roller coaster of Game Six finally ended. But the teams were back at it for Game Seven that evening. Boston jumped in front 3–0 in the third inning, but Perez' home run in the sixth brought the Reds close, and they tied it 3–3 in the seventh. Then in the ninth inning, with two outs and runners on first and third, Morgan hit a single into center field to put Cincinnati ahead. The Red Sox were out of comebacks. They went down in order in the bottom of the ninth inning, and the Reds were World Series champions.

Mob scene
The Reds had reason to celebrate after coming from behind to win Game Seven. It was their first World Series title since 1940.

Reds' Rose
Cincinnati third baseman Pete Rose was named the most valuable player of the 1975 Series after batting .370 in 27 at-bats.

23

1986: Curses!

In 1986, the "Curse of the Bambino" reared its ugly head in new and devious ways, when the N.L.'s New York Mets came from behind to beat the Red Sox in seven games. For Red Sox fans, Game Six remains one of the most painful examples of the dastardly spell that has been cast over their club. But first, a little background is in order. The Boston Red Sox were perhaps baseball's most successful franchise in the early 20th century. They won the first World Series in 1903, when they were known as the Boston Americans, then took four more titles by 1918. The last three of those championships came in a four-season span from 1915 to 1918, when the Red Sox featured a star pitcher and sometimes slugging outfielder named Babe Ruth.

Boston owner Harry Frazee was losing money in his theater business. So after the 1919 season, when Ruth became a nearly full-time outfielder and blasted a record 29 home runs, Frazee sold his star to the New York Yankees for a wad of cash. Unfortunately for the Red Sox, Ruth went on to become one of the greatest players ever.

Business decision
Harry Frazee took some of the money he got from selling Ruth and put on Broadway musicals.

Season to remember
The 1986 squad was the first Mets' team since 1973 to play in the World Series. This booklet helped the press write about the team.

Good Knight
Third baseman Ray Knight (that's his helmet, above) scored the winning run in Game Six and homered in the Mets' win in Game Seven. He batted .391 in the Series.

Home, sweet home
Games Six and Seven of the 1986 Series were played at New York's Shea Stadium. The Mets moved into their home in 1964 and have played there ever since.

Starting with Ruth, the Yankees built the most successful club in baseball—and the Red Sox were saddled with the "Curse of the Bambino." As curses go, this one seems ironclad: the Red Sox have not won a World Series since they sold Ruth.

Now, on to 1986. New York was favored to take the Series, but the Mets quickly dropped the first two at home. They came back to win the next two games at Boston's Fenway Park before the Red Sox' Bruce Hurst won for the second time in Game Five. He went the distance in a 4–2 victory that pulled his team within one win of the world championship.

That win never came. In the fateful sixth game, which still haunts Red

Sox fans to this day, the teams battled to a 3–3 tie through nine innings. In the 10th, Dave Henderson's home run and Marty Barrett's single put Boston ahead 5–3. And when closer Calvin Schiraldi set down the first two Mets in the bottom of the inning, it looked like the curse would finally be broken.

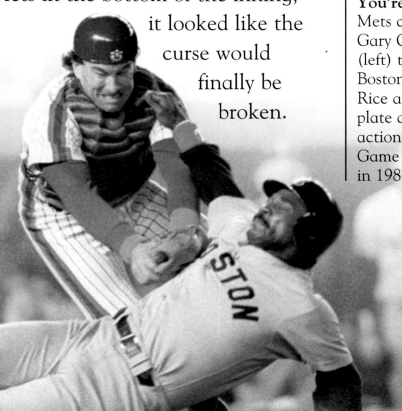

Oh-so-close
The Red Sox just missed ending their curse on several occasions. They lost Game Seven of the World Series in 1946, 1967, 1975, and 1986.

You're out!
Mets catcher Gary Carter (left) tags out Boston's Jim Rice at home plate during action from Game Six in 1986.

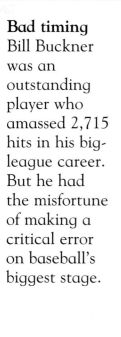

Bad timing
Bill Buckner was an outstanding player who amassed 2,715 hits in his big-league career. But he had the misfortune of making a critical error on baseball's biggest stage.

The celebratory champagne was on ice in the Red Sox' locker room, but New York's Gary Carter kept his team's faint hopes alive with a single. Kevin Mitchell followed with another single, then Ray Knight fell behind no balls and two strikes. The Mets were down to their very last strike. Knight's soft hit on the next pitch, though, fell into center field. Carter scored, pulling New York within one run, and Red Sox fans couldn't bear to watch. Veteran Bob Stanley came on to relieve Schiraldi and face outfielder Mookie Wilson. With the count two balls and two strikes, Wilson fouled off two pitches. The next pitch was inside—too far inside. It sailed to the backstop, and Mitchell raced home on the wild pitch. The score was tied at 5–5.

With the Shea Stadium crowd in a frenzy, Wilson fouled off the next two pitches. Then he hit a slow ground ball toward Bill Buckner at first base. To the horror of Red Sox fans everywhere, the ball trickled though Buckner's legs. Knight rounded third and scored without a throw. The Mets won, 6–5.

Fenway blues The Red Sox lost Game Seven at home in 1967 when they were shut down by Cardinals' ace Bob Gibson.

Greeting committee Howard Johnson (20) and the Mets were there to welcome Ray Knight (22), whose run won Game Six for the Mets.

The irony is that Buckner, who had an injured leg, normally would have been lifted for a defensive replacement once the Red Sox had taken the lead. In this case, though, Boston manager John McNamara wanted the veteran to be on the field for the first World Series celebration of his 18-year career. But the only celebration was by the Mets, who joyously danced around home plate, jumping up and down like kids on the playground.

For many people, Buckner's error essentially ended the Series, although the Red Sox once again teased their fans by taking a 3–0

Twice the fun
The Mets celebrated joyously after their dramatic victory in Game Six (left). They repeated the scene after their Series-clinching victory the next night.

Ten pitches
Boston's Bob Stanley and New York's Mookie Wilson battled for 10 pitches in the decisive at-bat of Game Six. With the count two balls and two strikes, Wilson fouled off two pitches. The seventh pitch was wild, scoring the tying run. After two more foul balls, Wilson hit the fateful grounder to Bill Buckner.

lead into the sixth inning of Game Seven. But the Mets followed with a barrage of runs to win, 8–5.

The finale was almost anticlimactic. After Game Six, it was as if the Series outcome was pre-planned. That's just silly, though, isn't it. There's not really such a thing as a curse . . . is there?

1991: Cinderella Story

The Cinderella story is an old one in sports. Just like the title character in the classic fable, a Cinderella team gets an invitation to the big dance—in baseball's case, it is the World Series—that takes most people by surprise. But will the clock finally strike midnight with a World Series loss for that team?

Native son Jack Morris, who was born in St. Paul, Minnesota, led the Twins to a World Series championship in his only season with his hometown club in 1991. Morris also helped the Detroit Tigers (1984) and Toronto Blue Jays (1992) to Series titles.

Well, the 1991 World Series was unique because it featured not one, but two Cinderella teams in the A.L.'s Minnesota Twins and the N.L.'s Atlanta Braves. Those squads kept fans guessing right to the very end which one of them the glass slipper would fit. Ultimately, it was the Twins who prevailed, four games to three, in one of the most suspense-filled World Series ever.

The Twins won 95 games in 1991 behind the pitching of Scott Erickson, Jack Morris, and closer Rick Aguilera. But they also had an offensive star in outfielder Kirby Puckett, who batted .319 and was a dynamic presence on the field and in the clubhouse.

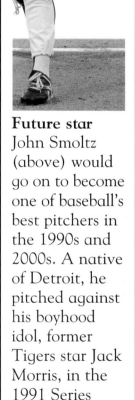

Future star
John Smoltz (above) would go on to become one of baseball's best pitchers in the 1990s and 2000s. A native of Detroit, he pitched against his boyhood idol, former Tigers star Jack Morris, in the 1991 Series finale. Smoltz was brilliant, but it wasn't enough.

Head-over-heels

Atlanta catcher Gregg Olson looks like he got the worst of this home-plate collision during Game One. But he held onto the ball after tagging out Dan Gladden. Plays like this made the 1991 Series nonstop entertainment.

Almost identical Twins

Minnesota won its first World Series in 1987, and the Twins did it in similar fashion to 1991—by winning four games at home, including Games Six and Seven, against the Cardinals.

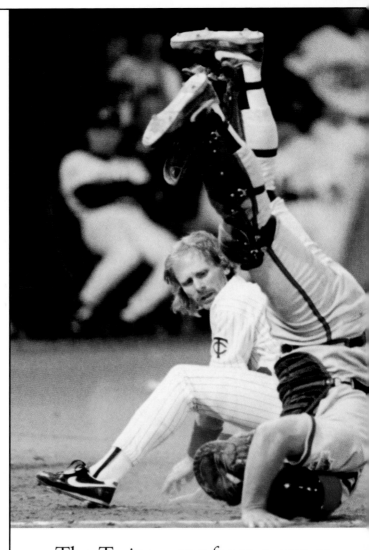

The Twins went from worst to first in the A.L. They were matched in the N.L. by the Braves, who improved from a major-league-low 65 wins in 1990 to 94 in 1991.

The two Cinderellas battled tooth and nail in a true Fall Classic.

Minnesota won the first two games at home, with their wildly enthusiastic fans waving white towels called "Homer Hankies" and nearly raising the roof of the Hubert H. Humphrey Metrodome. The Twins won Game Two 3–2 on Scott Leius' tie-breaking home run in the bottom of the eighth inning. That blast was a portent of things to come: all but one game the rest of the way was decided by one run—and in the home team's final at-bat.

Pennant fever
Minnesota and Atlanta played one of the most exciting Series in history.

Home, sweet dome
The Twins had a tremendous home-field advantage inside the raucous Metrodome (below). In fact, the home team won each of the seven games in the 1991 Series.

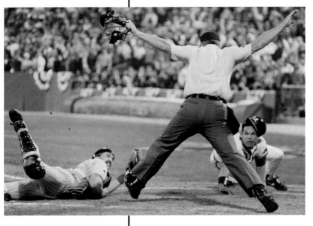

At home,
the Braves won
Game Three
5–4 in 12 innings
on light-hitting
Mark Lemke's
two-out single.

Close call
When David Justice (above, right) slid in safe at home in the 12th inning, the Braves won Game Three.

Then they tied the Series at two games each with a 3–2 win in Game Four when Lemke tripled and scored on a sacrifice fly in the bottom of the ninth. Game Five was the only breather in the Series. The Braves pounded out 17 hits in a 14–5 rout.

That set the stage for two of the most dramatic and entertaining games in World Series history.

Back at the Metrodome for Game Six, the Twins jumped out to a 2–0 lead in the first inning. The Braves came back to tie the game. The Twins went ahead again in the fifth inning. The Braves tied it again in the seventh at 3–3.

Homer hanky
No Twins' fan was without one in the Metrodome.

In the bottom of the 11th inning, Puckett, who had made a dramatic over-the-wall catch to take a homer away from Atlanta earlier, won it 4–3 with a leadoff homer.

Brave new world
Jack Morris of the Twins pitched a shoutout gem in Game Seven, much like Milwaukee Braves pitcher Lew Burdette's 5–0 blanking of the Yankees in the 1957 Series (above).

Big blast
The Twins' Kirby Puckett (left) rocked the Metrodome with a home run that won Game Six.

Special K
Sandy Koufax pitched a Game Seven shutout for the Dodgers in 1965. His three-hitter beat the Twins, 2–0.

It only seemed fitting that such a closely contested World Series should end with a closely contested final game. Morris took the mound in Game Seven for the Twins against the up-and-coming John Smoltz for Atlanta. The two battled for seven innings, matching zeros on the scoreboard all the way. In the eighth inning, the Braves had a great chance to score when they put runners on second and third with none out, but Morris shut the door.

In the bottom of the eighth, Smoltz gave way to his bullpen, but Morris continued to hold the Braves scoreless. Finally, in the bottom of the 10th, Dan Gladden dropped a hit into left-center field and hustled his way into second base with a leadoff double. Chuck Knoblauch sacrificed him to third base. With one out, the Braves elected to walk the next two batters and load the bases to set up a force play at any base. But pinch-hitter Gene Larkin lofted a hit to left field. Gladden danced home with the winning run, and bedlam erupted in the Metrodome!

Winning ball
Here's the ball that Gene Larkin hit for the game-winning single in the 10th inning of Game Seven.

Winning hit
With one out and the bases loaded in the bottom of the 10th inning, Gene Larkin (left) pinch hit for designated hitter Jarvis Brown. Larkin drilled the first pitch he saw for a base hit to drive home Dan Gladden with the Series-ending run.

2001: Goliath falls

The 2001 World Series was a classic case of David versus Goliath. It pitted the upstart Arizona Diamondbacks against the vaunted New York Yankees. In the end, David felled Goliath with one decisive swing of the bat in the bottom of the ninth inning, and the N.L.'s Diamondbacks won the Series, four games to three.

In truth, the Diamondbacks were not really an overachieving team. They won 92 games during the 2001 regular season with a well-balanced squad that combined the pitching of veteran fireballers Randy Johnson and Curt Schilling with the hitting of stars such as outfielder Luis Gonzalez. Still, Arizona was only in its fourth year—it was an expansion team in 1998—and had not yet built up any tradition. Meanwhile, the Yankees were, well, the Yankees. They had an all-time record 26 world championships, including three in a row and four in the previous five seasons. They boasted of more tradition than any place outside of Cooperstown.

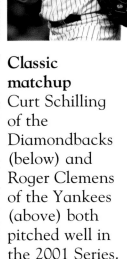

Classic matchup
Curt Schilling of the Diamondbacks (below) and Roger Clemens of the Yankees (above) both pitched well in the 2001 Series.

The Diamondbacks weren't intimidated in the face of all that history. Instead, they trotted out Schilling and Johnson in the first two games, which were in their home ballpark in Phoenix. If anything, it was the Yankees' hitters who were intimidated by all that power. Schilling and Johnson both were capable of throwing the ball about 100 miles per hour (160 kmh)! Schilling breezed through seven innings in the opener and won, 9–1. Johnson came right back the next night and tossed a three-hit shutout to win, 4–0. Suddenly, the Yankees' long reign as champions was in jeopardy. But don't count them out yet! At home for Game Three, they won 2–1 behind future Hall of Famer Roger Clemens' pitching. Then they won the next

two games in dramatic fashion.
With two outs in the bottom of the
ninth of Game Four, Tino Martinez
belted a game-tying, two-
run home run off young
Diamondbacks closer
Byung-Hyun Kim to
make it 3–3. Then
in the 10th, Derek
Jeter homered off
Kim to win it,
4–3, and even
the Series at
two games
apiece.

Korean import
Diamondbacks
closer Byung-
Hyun Kim
(above) became
the first
Korean-born
player in the
World Series.

**Time to
celebrate**
Derek Jeter's
winning home
run in the
bottom of the
10th inning of
Game Four
(left) capped
New York's
rally and tied
the Series.

Deja vu
One night after Tino Martinez tied Game Four with a two-out, ninth-inning home run, Scott Brosius repeated the feat in Game Five.

Junior circuit
The first World Series upset came in the first World Series. The A.L.'s Boston Americans (right) stunned the Pittsburg Pirates of the N.L.

It was a brutal loss for Arizona. But unfortunately for the Diamondbacks, they would have to relive it again the very next night!

They took a 2–0 lead into the bottom of the ninth inning, when Kim faced New York's Scott Brosius with a man on base. Brosius lofted a high fly ball to deep left field. The ball cleared the wall for a home run, and the game was tied at 2–2. Three innings later, the Yankees pushed across a run to win, 3–2. Unbelievably, they led the Series, three games to two. No team in history had ever won back-to-back Series games in which they trailed entering the ninth. Chalk up another one to Yankees' lore.

Most teams would have crumbled in the face of such adversity. But Arizona was going back home. Plus, the Diamondbacks knew they had saved Johnson for Game Six. The "Big Unit," as he is called, pitched seven innings, but Arizona's bats took over in a 15–2 rout. The Series was tied.

What a relief
Randy Johnson won Game Seven by coming out of the bullpen after winning Games Two and Six as a starter.

Souvenir item
Arizona stars Luis Gonzalez and Curt Schilling signed this base (above) from Game One. Gonzalez and Schilling also both played pivotal roles in Game Seven.

Desert swarm
Arizona Diamondbacks players (right) exult in their come-from-behind victory over the New York Yankees in the seventh, and final, game of the Series.

Clemens and Schilling squared off in Game Seven, a nail-biting pitchers' duel. The Diamondbacks broke a scoreless tie with a run in the sixth, but the Yankees scored a run in the seventh, then took a 2–1 lead in the eighth before Johnson, who had just pitched the night before, came on to shut the door.

Speaking of shutting the door, that was Yankees closer Mariano

Rivera's specialty. No reliever in big-league history ever has had as much success in the World Series as Rivera. But like just about everything else in this exciting Series, the Diamondbacks refused to bow to history. Mark Grace led off the ninth with a single. Then Rivera made an error on a sacrifice attempt. After an out, Tony Womack doubled to tie the score at 2–2. Then, with the bases loaded, Luis Gonzalez dropped a single into left-center field. Jay Bell scored the winning run as Gonzalez leaped for joy on his way to first base. Arizona had won 3–2 and toppled baseball's Goliath!

Jump for joy
Diamondbacks outfielder Luis Gonzalez exults after his game-winning hit in the bottom of the ninth inning of Game Seven.

Miracle Mets
One of the biggest World Series upsets came in 1969, when the Mets, heavy underdogs to a seasoned Baltimore team, won in five games.

Glossary

ace
An informal name for a team's best starting pitcher

adversity
Difficult circumstances or hardships to overcome

American League (A.L.)
The younger of the two groups of teams that make up the major leagues. (It is sometimes called the "Junior Circuit.") There are currently 14 teams in the American League, which began play in 1901.

blooper
In baseball, it's a softly hit ball that carries over the infielders but drops in front of the outfielders.

closer
A relief pitcher who is used almost exclusively to finish games ("close" them) while protecting his team's small lead of one, two, or three runs

expansion team
A new franchise that starts from scratch, thus increasing ("expanding") the number of teams in a given league

finale
The final occurrence of something, usually a game or performance

foul pole
The tall, metal pole that extends above the outfield fences directly down the right- and left-field lines on a baseball field. The foul pole helps umpires determine if a ball hit over the fence is fair or foul. (A ball that hits the foul pole is, oddly, fair.)

goat
Someone who is blamed for something that goes wrong

grand slam
A home run that comes with the bases loaded

jeopardy
In danger, or at risk of losing something

National League (N.L.)
The older of the two groups of teams that make up the major leagues. (It is sometimes called the "Senior Circuit.") There are currently 16 teams in the National League, which began play in 1876.

portent
An indication of something that is about to occur

prelude
An introduction to something more important that is to follow

preordained
Something that has already been determined in advance

reprieve
Relief from some harm or punishment

routine
Normal or regular. A routine fly ball is one that usually would be caught with ease.

scenario
An outline of events

underdog
An individual or team that is expected to lose or to fail

upstart
Someone or something that suddenly is raised to a position of importance

vaunted
Something boasted of or bragged about

walk-off home run
A home run that puts the home team ahead in the bottom of the ninth inning or in extra innings, thus automatically ending the game (the teams "walk off" the field)